Gray Wolves

by Mary Meinking

Consultant:
Blaire Van Valkenburgh
Professor
UCLA Department of Ecology and Evolutionary Biology

New York, New York

Credits

Cover and Title Page, © Wolf Mountain Images/Shutterstock; 4–5, © A.von Dueren/ Shutterstock; 6–7, © Dennis Donohue/Shutterstock; 8–9, © Getty Images/Jupiter Images/Thinkstock; 10–11, © StanTekiela.com; 12–13, © Minden Pictures/SuperStock; 14, © Pesat Jaroslav/Shutterstock; 14–15, © FLPA/SuperStock; 16–17, © Animals Animals/ SuperStock; 18–19, © Critterbiz/Shutterstock; 20–21, © BiosPhoto/SuperStock; 22T, © Dennis Donohue/Shutterstock; 22C, © Critterbiz/Shutterstock; 22B, © Irantzu Arbaizagoitia/Shutterstock; 23T, © Brenda Carson/Shutterstock; 23B, © Pesat Jaroslav/ Shutterstock.

Publisher: Kenn Goin
Senior Editor: Joyce Tavolacci
Creative Director: Spencer Brinker
Design: Becky Daum
Photo Researcher: Arnold Ringstad

Library of Congress Cataloging-in-Publication Data

Meinking, Mary.
  Gray wolves / by Mary Meinking ; consultant, Blaire Van Valkenburgh.
    p. cm. — (Wild canine pups)
  Audience: 6–9.
  Includes bibliographical references and index.
  ISBN 978-1-61772-926-3 (library binding) — ISBN 1-61772-926-4 (library binding)
  1. Gray wolf—Infancy—Juvenile literature. 2. Wolves—Infancy—Juvenile literature.
I. Van Valkenburgh, Blaire. II. Title.
  QL737.C22M438 2014
  599.773—dc23
                                                2013008959

For more information, write to Bearport Publishing Company, Inc., 45 West 21st Street, Suite 3B, New York, New York 10010. Printed in the United States of America.

10 9 8 7 6 5 4 3 2 1

🐾 Contents 🐾

Meet gray wolf pups

It is springtime in a forest.

Two gray wolf pups leave their **den** for the first time.

The eight-week-old pups are very small.

However, they will grow quickly.

In one year, they will be as big and strong as their parents.

den

gray wolf pups

What is a gray wolf?

Gray wolves live in the northern parts of the world.

They are the largest kind of **canine**.

Their size makes them good hunters.

They hunt deer, elk, and moose.

North America
Atlantic Ocean
Europe
Asia
Pacific Ocean
Africa
Pacific Ocean
South America
Indian Ocean

N
W E
S

☐ **Where gray wolves live**

adult gray wolf

Adult gray wolf size

Wolf packs

Gray wolves live in family groups called packs.

A pack may have more than 20 adults and pups.

Each pack has a male and a female leader.

The adults in a pack work together to hunt for prey and care for young pups.

gray wolf pack

Inside a den

In the spring, a mother wolf makes a den in a cave or in a hillside.

Inside the den, she gives birth to four to six pups.

Each baby weighs only one pound (0.45 kg).

The mother curls her body around her tiny pups to keep them warm.

gray wolf mother

gray wolf pups

11

Newborn pups

For the first three weeks of their lives, the pups cannot see or hear.

During this time, the mother wolf stays in the den with her babies.

She protects them from **predators**, such as coyotes.

If an enemy comes near, the mother will growl.

If the enemy comes even closer, she may attack.

Time to eat

A wolf pup's first food is its mother's milk.

When the pups are a few weeks old, they start eating meat.

Adult wolves in the pack hunt **prey** to feed the babies.

adults hunting prey

They swallow the meat and carry it back to the den.

Then the adults spit up the soft meat for the pups to eat.

adult spitting up meat

pup eating

Staying safe

Pups stay near the den for safety.

When they hear or smell an enemy, the pups hide inside.

adult guarding pups

pup in den

Pups also rely on the adults in their pack to protect them.

While the other wolves go hunting, one adult guards the pups.

Wolf signals

The growing pups use their bodies to **communicate** with the pack.

If a wolf wants to play, it lowers its head and wags its tail.

If a wolf is afraid, it holds its tail between its legs.

pup lowering its head

19

Growing up

When the pups are ten months old, they hunt with the adults.

As the adult wolves catch prey, the pups watch and learn.

When they are one year old, the pups are fully grown.

They have learned all the skills they need to hunt with the pack!

gray wolf pack

21

❖ Glossary ❖

canine (KAY-nyen)
a member of the dog
family, which includes pet
dogs and gray wolves

communicate
(kuh-MYOO-nuh-kayt)
to pass on information

den (DEN)
a home where
animals can rest, hide
from enemies, and
have babies

predators
(PRED-uh-turz)
animals that
hunt and eat
other animals

prey (PRAY)
animals that
are hunted and
eaten by other
animals

Index

Read more

Fink Martin, Patricia A. *Gray Wolves (True Books: Animals).* New York: Children's Press (2002).

Lawrence, Ellen. *A Wolf's Life (Animal Diaries: Life Cycles).* New York: Bearport (2012).

Simon, Seymour. *Wolves.* New York: HarperCollins (2009).

Learn more online

To learn more about gray wolves, visit
www.bearportpublishing.com/WildCaninePups

About the author

Mary Meinking is the author of 23 nonfiction children's books. She works as a graphic designer during the day. In her spare time, Mary enjoys traveling, photography, crafts, and writing for children. She lives with her family on a lake in northwest Iowa where she watches wildlife year-round.